The Extreme Dream

Robert Boyd Knott

Edition: First Edition

ISBN: 979-8893975444

Published by EliteScribes Book Writing

Table of Contents

Foreword

In 2003, rather than show up for work and help my Dad like I said I would, I decided to party and get high on ecstasy. The next day, my Dad was nowhere to be found. Later that day, my Mom and I found his car on a back country road. He had shot himself with a shotgun, he was unrecognizable. Time stopped, and I was completely devastated; it felt as if he had killed me, too. I carried extreme guilt, shame, and anger, and for many years, I couldn't forgive myself, nor could I forgive God. This event altered my trajectory, though I don't know if I was going anywhere anyway, considering how I was living.

It's very complicated. I grew up in an extreme environment. I always had a roof over my head and clothes on my back, and I never went hungry; my Dad made sure of that. He was also very old school and a workaholic. My Mom was a very talented writer who struggled with her mental health. She would leave to go to a mental health facility sporadically while I was a child.

I had three different nannies; two were black women from Jamaica, and one was a young white woman who I learned very quickly could not be trusted. In many ways, I grew up with an extreme amount of freedom and was unsupervised during a lot of early childhood. It was both incredible and terrifying.

These writings or poems came from a very dark, surreal, lonely place. Somehow, they transformed into something else, I have decided to share them. Some of them have nothing to do with pain or loss and are innocent of those dark times, while others could only be conceived because of those dark times.

I love my parents; they did the best they could, and we had many great times, too; it was just, at times, extreme and very confusing. And this is how the extreme became a dream, and coal was turned into diamonds, for lack of a better analogy.

Any revenue this book generates, 20% will go to a charity for PTSD and people suffering from trauma. The rest will go towards my son's education. This is dedicated to my parents and to my friends and family. Thank you for your unwavering support over the years, I thank God for you.

Love,
Rob

I was born into this world and the world gave me its inexperience, its anxiety, its self-projection, its loneliness, anger, and its hate. I was a hungry innocent child and I swallowed it all by mistake.

Endeavor

Photo Credits: Daniel Roberts

To be a man of few words
and kind ones when spoken.
And to take good action consistently
towards that which is both unexpected and chosen.

To replace sympathy with empathy
and judgment with love,
and to think myself no better than anyone else,
neither below or above.

To be of good service and good cheer
through all weathers and circumstances,
to not take too seriously my victories or defeats,
whether I lose ground or advance.

To do the best with what I have
wherever I happen to be,
to remember that life is more than what I do,
it's in the now — just being me.

To go my own way,
oblivious to whether it's considered right or wrong
by my family or peers,
trusting my own heart and instincts
when the way is filled with obstacles
despite both rational and irrational fears.

To narrow my focus
and go all out for and towards who and what I love the
most,
to let go and surrender
as faith allows me to climb as I relax and coast.

To be free of both the past
and future uncertainty,
to rise above and go beyond
self-imposed limitations with intention and sincerity.

And I'm there, against all odds,
despite all setbacks,
in gratitude for what I had considered unforgivable.

Robert Knott

The Void

When I lost you
it was almost as if I didn't know myself anymore.
The pain was immense,
and the sadness I felt left me stranded on a distant
shore.

Things became clichés,
quotes, cautionary tales,
and a great excuse.
Time doesn't heal all wounds;
sometimes it burns you up
and leaves you in a heap of ashes
among the detritus and refuse.

One day,
you pick up the pieces
and you make yourself a collage.
You glue yourself back together
based on thoughts of who you used to be
and the delirious hope found in a mirage.

You smile
'cause you can't give circumstance the pleasure,
and you're too brave or stupid to quit.
You come out the other side
because there was more love for life
than you could ever remit.

Burned Into the Soul

Your deepest feelings grow old with you,
changing as you change through the years,
alive in their bitterness and joy,
alive in their pain and laughter,
alive and changing with your perception.

They are burned into your soul.
When you can barely remember your own name
and who you are,
they are still with you,
like good friends who've stood the test of time
and sworn eternal enemies.

There's no forgetting what's grown
and taken root within your own soul.
There's only denial and acceptance,
and different kinds of tears.

In a Dark Room

A machine clamors to help an old man get more oxygen,
it sounds like steel being pressed over and over,
which is strange if you think about it.

Or like a train braking
as it stops to take you to your final destination.
I don't know.
I've given up trying to know.

Now I'm just a translator,
but of what I can't exactly say.
Only that I am able to channel something
so that it can be more easily absorbed,
imagined, or grasped.
For what reason,
I don't really know —
only that I can do it.

So the translation begins...

I no longer know where I am
or who I'm with.
The lights are low,
and I'm plugged in
or maybe still connected in a way I don't understand.

I've got this great spirit that still yearns to stand,
though my legs aren't cooperating, damn.
Thankfully, I'm not alone,
there's a man I recognize,
but his name escapes me.

I think he might be an angel.
He just smiles and says,
"Not quite, just a good friend."

My breath is like a heavy fog
where the heat rises off the cold ground
in the beautiful early morning light,
the approaching sun signaling the promise of a new day,
yet somehow I know
the sun will soon set on me.

I can hear a train braking
slowly over and over again.
I will soon be ready.

I am bound for glory
and hope to soon be seeing
my wife, my brother, my sister, my dogs, and my parents.

There's lots of love for me here,
but I think there's even more
on the other side of this barrier between worlds.

The Old Lion

He's not what he once was,
but he can't see it.
He just knows the hunger and the instinct is there
and that this is his kingdom.

He's not as quick or strong as he once was,
but he doesn't know it.
Can't know it.
Will only truly know it
when he's bleeding out and close to death,
and maybe not even then.

In his prime,
he was magnificent —
a terrifying beast that couldn't be defeated,
couldn't be fathomed
by those that would challenge his rule.

He dispatched opponents with ease,
with grace and style
that almost belied a casual annoyance.
He loved to fight.
He *was* the fight,
and even in death,
he *is* the fight.

That Old Lion was special.
He did things other lions couldn't do.
He was just simply amazing.

It was his heart,
his soul,
and his hunger to dominate
and be the king of his realm.

That Old Lion
was the greatest lion to ever do it.
And yet his reign is at its end,
his territory about to be seized,
and his body laid to rest
as nature takes its course.

And I can't help but feel sad
for that Old Lion
because I'm getting older too,
and I don't want to see it
and I don't want to know it.

I want that Old Lion
to win one more time
and then again
& again.

Again.

In My Heaven

In my Heaven,
I'll be able to right my wrongs,
put your light in my heart where it belongs,
and you'll be able to feel and see the real me,
and you'll know it was true—
the way I felt for you.

How, when it came to sacrifice,
I was ready and willing to pay the ultimate price.
And if that wasn't true,
how I prayed for God to take me away from you.

In my Heaven,
my friends and family are dressed in the most graceful light,
and everyone's in their prime.
There's a universal understanding and acceptance
that illuminates what's right—that's sublime.

And we realize that it's our differences
that make us beautiful,
and there's no hate,
just a mutual respect for love and truth
that radiates from the windows of our souls.

In my Heaven,
I'm able to protect the ones that I love
that are still breathing
and living without control.

And I can love them unconditionally,
and there's no judgment to pass or receive,
just admiration for the spiritual
as I can finally see my people and believe
that they truly are pure light.

And I smile,
for I can still feel their warmth
on the coldest and loneliest of nights,
from their energy that emanates and shines
from a hundred million miles away—
just like an exploding star.

In my Heaven,
I have finally found peace.
So don't be sad or cry for me.

And even though it may seem like I'm gone,
celebrate and be happy
in that I am finally free.

And rest assured knowing
that in my Heaven,
there's no place
that docsn't exist
without you in it.

In Order to Survive

(Message to Ghosts)

I had to detach from my thoughts and emotions,
or they were going to overwhelm and drown me.
I had to let go of the past and not worry about the future,
or I would never sleep soundly.

I had to focus on my son and what was right
instead of what I judged to be wrong
in order to laugh and smile.
I had to embrace the pain and stay with it,
for I could no longer mask it or live in denial.

I had to stop and really listen to the sounds of nature
so I could rediscover the joy of stillness and silence.
I had to turn off the media
so I could get away from all the sex, drugs, and violence.

I had to take the time I needed for myself
to heal and relearn to be alone.
I had to cultivate more love for myself
than I had ever previously known.

I had to go deep within myself
to find the cure and the reason.
I had to love and fight for my true self
every day through every changing season.

I had to acknowledge that I was talented,
blessed,
and needed to show more love and gratitude.
I had to get over myself
with sheer determination and a vigilant positive attitude.

I had to both forget and remember who I was
in order to know which way to go.
I had to be victorious and also surrender
in ways the world will never really know.

I had to swallow my selfish pride
and learn how to ask for more help.
I had to drink both bitter and joyful tears
that told the truth of how I really felt.

I had to relearn how to hope and trust
that my faith wouldn't shatter
should disaster strike again.
I had to learn to keep both my heart and mind open,
no matter the "what, if, how, why, or when."

I had to drink more water, exercise,
and eat healthy on a regular basis.
I had to redevelop the four pillars
of my soul's homeostasis.

I had to become more mindful of my actions
and more consciously aware.
I had to increase my faith in all that is
by returning to God and prayer.

Silent Crossing

A lazy cat sleeping in the sun

An old man lighting up another one

A real stillness on a beautiful country day

And there might not be another better way

Nature sings its favorite primordial song

And for a glorious moment, there's nothing wrong

An unforced smile is bestowed upon my face

Clear blue sky can't find a cloud any damn place

There's a cool, gentle breeze that's a gift and a blessing

Nothing like a quiet grace to keep a man from stressing

Light glistens on the leaves of an old majestic heritage oak

And there's respite from a world that sometimes feels mad and broke

Caged Tiger

There's a place where every smile
is a courageous and fearless act.
Where burdens are denied
but backs and legs are strong as fuck.

A place that is far away and forgotten,
and so close to your heart
that it's a part of you forever.
It's a place that you both dream about
and hope to escape from.

It's a beautiful reality
and a horrible nightmare
that oscillates between your joy,
pain, love, hate,
freedom,
and imprisonment.

One and the Same

A man falls through the cracks,
and he beats his dead horse,
he's trying to beat it back alive.

It's hopeless to be sure,
he doesn't know what else to do.
He loves that horse—
it gives him every excuse
but the right one.

Time folds back on itself,
and the colt sees the boy for the first time.
The boy knows it's going to be
a long and painful journey,
but the colt's ready to run,
and the boy's ready to ride.

Oliver the Octopus

My Octopus is smarter than your dog
and better than your cat.
Let me break it down,
I'll give you the facts.

He's got 8 arms, nine brains and 3 hearts,
he's got them both beat
and that's just the start.

His name is Oliver,
he lives in our saltwater swimming pool,
he has jet propulsion—
you have to admit that's pretty cool.

He can also change colors
and rapidly alter his shape,
I mean that's like superhero stuff—
maybe I'll get him a cape.

He could wear sunglasses and fight crime,
he could wrap up criminals with his tentacles—
I think it's just a matter of time.

You'll probably see him on the news pretty soon
for stopping bank robbers with his ink,
it'll read,
"Octopus blinds gang, then carries them to clink"

I don't think there's any dogs or cats
that could compete or do all that.
If you find one, let me know
so I can tip my hat,

but until then
I'll take my Octopus
over your dog or cat.

Texas

My blood is in its ground,
and its rivers carry familial dust,
ashes, and my heart with its blessings and burdens
out to sea.

The rusted pump jacks languidly rising and falling,
silhouetted against the marigold sky,
as the thunderhead rolls in.

Its backroads and old highways
covered in wildflowers that Van Gogh and Monet
could only see in their dreams and would have killed for,
the coastal wetlands at sunrise
so glorious it would make the devil himself
want to become a fisher of men,

the battle cry that still echoes
in the soul of its republic and its people,
the country girl that picked its cotton
and rested in the bar ditch on her way to school,
whose Daddy would do anything for anybody.

The bayous and spillways
explored with my brother
where we'd skip rocks and torment crawdads,
the small country town
and the beautiful young girl
who captured my heart and virginity,

the wind-swept Spanish oaks and bald cypresses
that rustle and whisper
the apologies and reprimands of ghosts.

The myriad of hues painted on its horizon
that remind a body
that hope and change is still possible,
the old man sitting in the old truck

with the blue heeler resting his head in his lap
as he sips a beer in the shade
and pulls on a cigarette.

...This poem will forever be unfinished
just like my love for Texas.

The Vivid Dream

The smell of jasmine
from that long-lost concrete jungle
floods the memories of a cornered youth.

Rocks would fly at hornets' nests,
we'd run, laugh,
and wince at the pain from our brave stupidity,
and then we'd do it again.

Vacant houses,
vandalism,
and the freedom of destruction.

The spillways, ditches, and bayous
with their littered tires and us,
with our sticks and rocks,
tormenting the crawdads in silent reverence
as rare moments in time
were unknowingly suspended.

Exploration of urban decay—
and what was there,
what it truly is,
and what it meant—
is too beautiful to describe with words
and defies explanation.

The beat of worn-out shoes
rapidly hitting the street
and fading into the distance
as we outran ourselves
and escaped the very real consequences
of danger,
capture,
and the rules.

My

My hopes are tied to dreams
that will never die,

my heart's fastened
to wind-filled sails and wings that fly,

my mind's alive and open
to the possibility that there are doors
and spirit worlds in the eye,

and my soul stirs to music
that lifts my spirits and takes me high,

my eyes reflect
the sun's beautiful truth
and the devil's terrible lie,

my hands hold the keys to vice and change
as they both welcome and wave goodbye,

my bones are infused
with questions of if, how, and why?

My body aches
from the pain and pleasure
of love that continues to fail and try,

my feelings crash like rogue waves
and rocket through ceilings
towards the sky,

and my experiences would make
even the hardest,
most unfeeling gangster
laugh and cry.

Freedom in Relativity

Music fills up the space,
taking you back to a different time,
a different place.

How far you've come,
it's difficult to think back
on when you felt so lost, so numb.

Nostalgia isn't always what it's cracked up to be,
yet you survived
and feel lucky.

Wide spectrums, polar opposites,
and all-or-nothing extremes,
lots of terrible nightmares
and beautiful dreams.

Acceptance and letting go,
I learned so many things
you never really wanted to know.

Smiling even though you felt sad,
and even using denial
to convince yourself that things weren't that bad.

You did what you had to
by any means necessary
to keep hope alive,
you head out west with your brother
and just drive.

Ecosystems change,
clouds disperse like thoughts and feelings,
and there's freedom
once you're out of range.

Blessed to be breathing
in this beautifully strange fragile miracle,
the data is flawed
but your instincts and knowledge
are more or less empirical.

You give your gift to the world
without too much second thought,
people remember what you gave,
not what you bought.

Time is your greatest asset—
more valuable than any material thing—
when you've really lost
is also when you win everything.

Sometimes you question reality
and you're overcome with doubt,
you pray that your love and faith
is greater than what you've become fearful about.

Don't give up,
cut yourself some slack,
just head towards who and whatever you love,
smile,
and focus on that.

Vertigo

Thinking myself out of this trap
we call society.

I can't help but think
they've lied to me.

Selling me a fake dream
of a better life just around the corner,
there's my ghost
arguing with the coroner.

Freedom and love,
my only desire,
watching as my ashes
are cremated in the fire.

Did I honor myself
by doing my own thinking?
Did I rise higher
and leave this place better than I found it?

Or did I just smile,
resigned to my fate
as my ship was sinking,
killing the pain of my life
with more smoking and drinking?

Hopefully,
I denied their programming and my own.
Still,
I feel the music of my life and my soul,
and it's jamming something full-grown.

Smiling at the end,
knowing deep down
all this material bullshit
is just paper in the wind,

and that love
was the only reason.

Looking to the sky,
contemplating the moon and the stars,
wondering why.

Without

Without a way to make you smile,
something will be eternally missing from my life

Without a way to tell you the truth,
something will forever not be right

Without a way to give you everything that you need
is not a way I could continue

Without a way to see myself
I could never see you and do any better

Without a way to bridge the gap,
it's not a way I want to go,
it's too far away from you.

Together

Bloody rags holding war torn soldiers
together, we can make it.

Come on brother,
don't let them steal your life away.

Blood rags holding war torn soldiers
together, it's hell today.

Hear our train coming,
that's our ticket out of here.

Come on brother,
it's time to go,
we gotta let 'em know,
we won't die, we're gonna live,
that's right,
can't see us falling,
can't see us crawling...

As we pull ourselves up out of the ashes,
recovering from the torn limbs and plane crashes...

In the distance, I see bloody rags and war torn soldiers
standing... together.

On the Mend

Life is pain,
facing your troubles head-on
with your honor intact—
that's how you play the game.

There's gonna be tragedy,
regret, anguish, and shame,
you fight through that shit
and smile at your dark clouds all the same.

I remember you and me
dancing in the parking lot to the music
when it was pouring down rain
and nothing could shut our joy down,

golden moments shining through angry skies
and our hope was all around.

I can feel light welling up
and rising inside me again after all this time,
fighting for self-change,
defying darkness,
and suddenly it's all sublime.

I realize that even though I had been lost,
I can still come back against all odds and win,
surviving by adaptation
through nonstop determination,
sacrifice, and discipline.

I start to run
and I push to pick up the pace,
feeling kind of like a clouded leopard
that's stalking victory,

motivated by hunger
in a fucked up rat race.

And all I know
is that this world better fucking watch out,
cause I'm done with all the guilt,
anger,
self-destruction
and doubt.

Can you feel me?
Really feel me shining like a sun?
Or do you have to see me bleed
for the sins of everyone?

Is there nothing I can do,
to help you get what you need?
I hope you know
I'd like nothing better
than to one day see you get free.

And as for me,
well—
sometimes you have to break
before you can bend,
it took a long time to heal,
but I'm finally on the mend.

Nothing is Knowing a Thing

As much as they need your light,
they need some of your darkness too.

They need to look into you,
and see what can't be brought to light,
so they can connect
on a level that's not easily understood.

You fail yourself,
and you know all you can do is keep going.

How much of your work
gets done, then undone?
Most of it,
if you're honest with yourself.

We try to control
what can't be controlled.
Teach me a lesson I'll never learn.
I'll have won,
lost,
and broken even
some other way.

Whatever happens, happens.
I'm not concerned
with the way you think I should be,
and you're not how I think you should be either—
but I'm willing to bet
we're both capable of better.

You're going to do what you feel,
not necessarily what you should,

and that's easy to relate to
'cause I'm human too.

Imperfect and smiling.
Imperfect and too strong
to let these tears fall—
it's just allergies.

I'm fine.
I'm better than I ever was,
and I'm worse too.

If you knew how I felt
you would pause,
you'd listen to the silence
tell you everything I couldn't say.

You'd read between the lines
and know I can't be saved
by what worked for you
or your rules,
but your prayers still make me feel good.

A purveyor of laughter
and good feeling—
that's really all I ever wanted to be.

I see a blinding light
shining with intensity,
and I'm pretty sure
it's both of us.

Out of Mind

Observing more
and judging less

Thinking less
and feeling more

Inundated with stimuli
and detaching from the mind,
the past,
the future...
only right now
is available
and meaningful

Egoism versus consciousness—
the state of the world
is a reflection of this

The channel and the source,
vibrant and also closed...
time is of the mind,
the mind is only a tool

Intention to open the heart...
I am a being of light
that harbors some darkness

Stillness and silence...
your home isn't your house,
it's your body

One's thoughts,
whether good or bad,
are ultimately just temporary

The present moment
is filled with grace
if you'd just allow yourself
to be free
of thought
and distraction.

Day of Birth

It's every day
It's a fight for the morning sun
It's opening yourself up to the power of One

It's the realization
that life's greatest gift is the present moment
and it's all you have

It's being of service to your fellow man,
and when they're hurting, applying the salve

It's the transformation of pain into joy
and hate into love

It's your heartfelt prayers
as you seek the grace and guidance of God above

It's harnessing the wind
and handing over the reigns

It's the secret magic
that still exists in the world
that you can't explain

It's the relentless search
for the evolution of your best self

It's the benefit of the doubt
that you give everyone else

It's integrity in the moment of choice
as you stay mindful
and relax into uncomfortable situations

It's a forced smile
when you're stressed the fuck out
and have to trust in your best guesstimation

It's the desire to move thoughts into action
and create something beautiful and real

It's the removal of distractions
and focusing on what's really important,
as your resolve turns to steel.

Remember

Remember when things weren't so complicated,
you and me getting into trouble intoxicated,
living life just as fast as we could run.

Hiding in bushes,
jumping over fences,
tearing up shit for the fuck of it,
getting lost in the sun.

No concept of the law,
the craziest little bastards you ever saw.

I remember feeling like we couldn't be beat,
and we still can't.

We ruled the street,
and when things got broken
we didn't really care,
nothing could stop us.

We had no money
and we lived like kings,
I remember feeling like
we could do anything—
and we still can.

More Than Enough

More than an addict
succumbing to the love
of his own pain and pleasure.

More than the trauma
of things I had no control over.

More than a bum
with no ambition
and an aversion to work.

More than an automaton
content with distraction and comfort.

More than mediocre
cause it's all or nothing
and I came to both win and lose.

More than they thought—
and that's okay.

More than they remember—
cause it slips their mind.

Better than a King
cause I don't care to rule
anyone but myself.

Humble and confident
yet mindful of meaningless expectations
and judgments.

Smiling at loss,
wincing and smiling at abundance
and its responsibility.

Accepting the shadow,
accepting the light,

blinding with intensity
as I come out of a dark nothing...
emergent.

Surfing my own waves of emotion,
riding my own intellect,
battling my own ego
as I attempt to shed the masks.

I am the imagination of the self,
an expression of the universe
getting high on its own creation.

Limitless like an ever-expanding space,
rooted in the consciousness of a man
striving to be free of gravity.

Healing

Open...
unguarded...
ready to understand or die.

Taking leaps of faith
toward the unknown
and smiling at a threatening sky.

Freedom in your mind
and the intelligence of your heart
to transform the things
that wounded
and ripped you apart.

Make Your Moments

So you scratch and claw,
you're digging deep,
lost in thoughts beyond translation,

and you're tripping on the stairs
and you can't count all the steps,
oh, the revelation—
it strikes you where you sleep,

and there's no other viable option for happiness,
and you've only got yourself to defeat.

So you make your moments
as you steal the time,
then you break your hand
punching a clock that won't rewind.

You've only got yourself
to see you through the dark,
no one can show you the way,

and the only sound you can hear
is the beat from your own heart.

So you dive into yourself,
and the only thing that matters
is remaining true.

Relief from Grief

If I could make you feel what I do...
you'd smile and cry.

You'd breathe easy and relax.
You'd stop judging yourself so harshly.
You'd understand that this is your time.
There's never been another one like you.

You'd get free of worry
and embrace the moment.
Your time is worth more
than all the money in the world.

You'd be thankful,
humble,
and confident.

You'd dance for no reason.
You'd throw caution to the wind
and roll the dice.

Your faith in love and yourself
would be stronger than fear.

You'd have quiet moments
to yourself every day.
You'd do better
cause you knew better...

What Do You Do?

When you've done all you can do,
and you only have the lesser of the evils to choose from

When your deepest heartfelt prayers go unanswered
and everything feels over and done

When the one person you could always rely and count on
kills themself,
and now everything they told you growing up
feels like a fucking lie

When you see your Dad
looking back at you in the mirror,
and all you see is anger, regret, and sorrow—
so you shed some tears
and let out the world's biggest sigh

You remember the good
You smile
You forgive yourself and them
You laugh

You focus on the little things
that are actually the really big things

You hug your dog
or let your cat sit on your chest and purr

You do something kind
for the people who were never able to recover
because you know
that could easily be you,
and helping others
makes you feel good about yourself.

Spiritual Postcard from the Hereafter

We're drifting, floating downriver through the hill country back towards the ocean. My ashes and little pieces of bone mixed with my wife's. We've finally come to rest on an ocean shelf off the coast of Texas.

Not to brag but the plants and animals like us and have gravitated towards us. They're building, depositing, and working on growing a beautiful coral reef. From death to life and life to death, the energy transforms, and the cycle continues. We're just glad to be together, in love and peace, still radiant and connected in the spiritual world.

My wife and I had a bet about what happens when you die, turns out I was right and she was wrong. There's that familiar scowl and eye roll that makes me smile. It's weird being everywhere at the same time. Though you do feel the energy pull more in the places and people you longed for and loved the most. Not much else to say except "keep love in your heart, do your best, and don't give up."

Sincere Love,
Bob and Alva

Robert Knott

Perspective

I was never able to change anybody no matter how hard I tried. I was only able to change myself and that's been hard as hell.

I never liked politics, though I know I should care about it more than I do, so whether you're conservative or liberal that's up to you. We can label each other however we want, but that doesn't define us, what defines us is how we live, and how we treat one another.

I think about my son and worry about what kind of world this is going to be for him. I used to think I had the answers, the older I've gotten I see the duality in just about everything. People are mirrors that reflect.

Hate is a drug, and racism is a disease, it affects all colors, all creeds. Does a person even know they're addicted or know they're sick? And if so, do they even want to get better? He or she has to want to do it for themselves. As a general rule people don't seem to care about something until it happens to them, that's unfortunate because it could eliminate a lot of needless suffering.

Empathy is about placing yourself in someone else's shoes and imagining what it's like for them... that's not easy either, you have to step outside of yourself. But I bet you do it for your children, and you probably have done it for family members or your close friends. You tried to understand because you love them. What about somebody who can do nothing for you? What if you're wrong? What if they can help you in ways you can't imagine?

I find most of what I think are the right answers in just listening and watching my son. Innocent, joyous, pure, and unbelievably kind. I want to be more like him and less like me. He gave me new eyes and new hope, he made me care when I didn't care about hardly anything, and I've still got a long ways to go.

None of us are perfect, and none of us are incapable of doing better. We just have to want to. Most of us instinctively know right from wrong, it's just a matter of what's in our heart.

A long time ago my friend's Dad told me blame was a wonderful thing, I thought about his words... blame absolves you from responsibility. It may do that but it doesn't change anything.

Change is hard, the best things are never easy. People grow, change, and heal at their own rates. You can't force somebody to get well, you can only pray for them, try to help them, and try to get to your very best. A great perspective normally takes a person their whole life.

I wish I was more patient, but there have also been times when I was damn near a statue... that's duality. Our best fluctuates depending on what we feel and what we think. No one can make you feel a certain way, that's a decision and a choice that we make ourselves.

It helps me to clarify my thoughts by writing them down, I'm sharing them because I need to be vulnerable. I'm way more closed off than you might realize, but I'm trying to open myself up.

My parents and grandparents are dead, I can no longer disappoint them or make them proud. I can only attempt to make myself proud, my son proud, my family proud, and my friends proud. I know I can do better and I am going to.

R.A.W

You were so thrilled,
left my heart overflowing.
It was more than filled.

Emotional waves
damn near drown,
accepting loss
as random tears still roll down.

Sometimes it feels
like there's something broken in my chest,
like you put too much in there,

and all I can do
is smile at the joy and pain
inside this chamber
with its drum that beats in defiance.

So I just focus my best on breathing air,
infinite moments flash in my mind,
and I know I have to stay in the present—
yet there's this big part of me
that just wants to hit rewind.

Faith tells me
that you knew how important
and beautiful you really were / are,
you gave me life
and helped a son
to feel like a star.

Transitory

Life is transitory
as well as infinite

Death is transitory
as well as infinite

Degrees measured by separation
Degrees measured by unification

Compassion, patience, and kindness—
to find peace and forgiveness,
to feel
and recognize all that is truly beautiful

Truth in one's eyes,
trust in one's touch,
love in one's heart,
and belief in one's soul

Know that the end
is the beginning

Know that there is no light without dark,
no peace without war,
and no love without hate

Accept change,
let go,
and give.

The Bird in my Beard

There's a bird that lives in my beard.
His name is Jimmy Reardon,
which is really pretty weird.

Cause he doesn't even like baseball,
and that's not even the strangest part,
no, not at all.

He pops out every hour on the hour,
and then he says
"I want gummy bears but only if they're sour."

And if I don't have any,
you know what he does?
He jumps out on my nose,
and threatens to peck off all my clothes.

I swear that Jimmy Reardon is really cray cray,
he goes cuckoo
almost every single day.

The way he moves his head
from side to side when he talks,
then he stops and starts again...

I say,
"Hey Jimmy, that's a balk."

But he pays me no mind,
he only wants gummy bears—
the sour kind.

Robert Knott

Right Now

Love is growing
and hate is being transformed into something better
by light that knows better.

It's raining on the drought,
and the land is getting wetter.

Things are not as bleak as they seem,
look to your gardens,
your knowledge,
your vision and dreams
that turn the dust and dirt
into something that's vibrant and green.

From hopelessness to prosperity,
there's a love that deals in miracles
and possibility.

Cynicism born in fear
has no life here,
it's played out and cannot win,
the beauty of truth
rises again and again.

Destruction is just a part of creation—
let your faith breathe life
into the winds of your soul's elation.

Shine your light
on this darkness and negativity,
it's up to you and me
to fight for a better day,
higher thoughts,
good feeling,
and levity.

Just relax,
everything is going to be as it should.

It's not how you thought,
but that should be expected
and understood.

The Way

The way the light sits on an oak leaf
or how it refracts
so that it appears as if there's a million diamonds
sparkling and glistening on the water

We should stop and really look and listen,
embrace the stillness and silence within ourselves,
breathe a sigh of relief—
we probably won't,
but we oughta

Everything that matters
is right here,
right now,
but we're worried about the future
or stranded in the past
and we don't let go,
not really

We want peace and freedom
but we seldom know how to go about it
We're locked in
and stuck out
and trapped
by whatever this is—
and it's maddening,
ridiculous,
and silly

We think we have more time
till death and loss slaps us in the face
and we're staring into a distance
a million miles away
and there's the deepest of sighs

Robert Knott

I'll Never Be the Same

Time doesn't heal all wounds—
some you just have to live with
They stay with you
for all your days

It's been hard to accept...
everything that's happened
It haunts me,
it interrupts my sleep,
and it makes me want to escape
to a place
where there's no memory

Wandering Free

It's now or never,
I'm ready to try,
I'm ready to die
for what I believe,

what's true is true...

I turn my head
like I turn the page,
I looked at past history
to see the future
that's raging out of control...

Tomorrow...
tomorrow needs a suture...

What do you do
trapped by biology,
governed by force—

do we have the strength
to make a change
and alter our course?

How much do we really need,
is there ever going to be enough?
Who's going to really try
to give something back
before we die,
who's going to bluff?

We can be cold
or we can play nice,
if it's true
then ante up and sacrifice

for a better world
for your fine son
or your beautiful girl,

love that makes you sick
you could hurl,

something beautiful,
a truth that's tragic,
a pain so deep
you could drown...

Now picture individuals
fighting to be free above ground,
now picture yourself
and really look at the ones you love—
see something so beautiful
it's impossible to describe...

Theory for Their Truth

They tried to box me in,
they had me dead to rights they figured,
but you can't outfox crazy,

and x don't always equal y.

The brain trust is a lacking,
and all the geniuses sigh.
They can keep a guessing—

I'm just the theory for their truth.

Watch 'em chase their tails,
playing possum,
threw 'em for a loop,

took 'em on a wild goose chase
all over God's green earth
and to hell and back
just to have a little fun.

See, when it comes down to survival
I ain't Darwin
but I ain't exactly dumb.

I'll take instinct
over intellect
every single time—
that's why they can't catch me
or find their damn proof.

They keep searching,
circling round,
running parallels
in the ceilings of their mind,

but I'm on the roof
getting blazed
and drinking,
quietly smiling
as I unwind.

Ode to the Self

I am love
I am light
I am peace
I am freedom

I am equanimity
I am acceptance of reality
I am detachment from overwhelming emotions

I am forgiveness
I am integrity in the moment of choice
I am denial of instant gratification
I am faith stronger than fear

I am transformation and change
I am discipline that's focused and consistent
I am clarity
I am relaxed, calm, and energetic

I am

Freedom

It lives inside you
and at the same time
you have to honor and cultivate it.

You have to let go of what you think you deserve
and concentrate on what you have to give.

It's worth dying for,
it's worth bestowing upon others,
it's worth more than any material thing.

It's what man/woman searches for...
to be free in who they are
and what they do.

It's music,
art,
it's your dog or cat,
it's your children at play—
showing and reminding you
that love is the answer

and the only place
that freedom is to be found
is deep in your heart and soul.

It's accepting
and letting go...
it's trusting yourself
and that higher power
that you are a part of...

it's denying yourself,
and it's beyond pleasure and pain.

Freedom is everything.

It's not needing to be liked
or understood.

It's so beautiful
that it's hard to describe
and it deserves to be celebrated every day...

I could go on and on.

I hope you have
more than you ever thought possible.

Life Happens...

And you're never the same...
The truth is
you're changing every day,
you just notice it more
when life throws you a curve.

The older I get
the more I realize
it doesn't matter what I say...
people are going to do
whatever they are going to do.

The only thing that matters
is that I don't let myself down,
that I stay true
to what I value most...

that I let love,
peace,
and freedom
reign supreme in my world.

Whatever This Is

Thank you...
for the relief and satisfying pleasure,
for the sharp and acute pain,
for the impossible love,
for the real hate,
for the swallowing darkness,
for the blinding light
that lets me know it's not too late.

Thank you...
for all the things I take for granted,
for the attachments,
for the new realizations,
for the breaking free,
for the discovery of the inner being
that's greater than my mind
that sometimes overtakes me.

Thank you...
for the uncompromising nature,
for the threatening and clear blue sky,
for the rain on my day off,
for the deep and vast oceans,
for the mountains that humble and stand alone,
for the flooding and lazy rivers,
for the inspiration and peace that they deliver.

Thank you...
for the isolation,
for the warm embrace,
for the elements,
for the freedom and the gravity,
for the Marianna Trench lows,
for the Mt. Everest highs,
for the simple beautiful truth
that radiates from a friend
and stranger's eyes.

Thank you...
for the euphoric and heartbreaking experiences,
for the stupid ass decisions,
for the lucky breaks I didn't deserve,
for the sinking ships,
for the miraculous rescues,
for the life-changing events
that threw me a curve
and hit me in both the heart and head,
for the fact that I am still here—
breathing,
smiling,
and not dead.

Thank you...
for the lies and deceit,
for the broken emptiness,
for the resolution,
for the incredible rebound,
for the golden silence,
for the lessons I wasn't meant to learn,
for the steel and sometimes liquid resolve,
for the dissolution of the former self
so that I could evolve.

Thank you...
for this selfishness,
for this generosity of spirit,
for this indifference,
for this overwhelming traumatic
and renewed creative feeling,
for the knowledge that imagination
can remove the illusion of a ceiling.

Thank you...
for the attention,
for the dismissal,
for the uncomfortable situations,

for the forgotten times,
for the surprise visit out of the blue,
for the many times
you were or weren't there
when I needed you.

Cherry Bend

Let it not be true,
that was my immediate thought,
yet I knew it was.

You were my brother from another mother...
I heard she's gone too.

Not sure what I feel,
feels like there should be tears,
we had history... years.

Regardless,
I'm gonna honor the real love I had for you.

I knew the real you
before the extracurricular got out of control.

I knew the kid
with the beautiful and contagious laugh.

I knew the kid
that gave no fucks,
who'd tell an adult straight up
"you fucking suck"
and it was the truth.

I knew the kid
who had unique skills at tennis,
who'd smoke adults on the court
and they'd be pissed off
because he was talking shit
and backing it up.

I knew the kid
who'd meet me outside on the street

after my parents fell asleep,
who'd up the ante,
double dog dare me,
who'd laugh so hard
he couldn't breathe.

I knew the kid
who had an ear for music
and couldn't wait to share it.

If there was a better instigator
or shit talker—
I'm not sure I've met your equal.

I remember a kid
who was brilliant
and could have done anything.

We were thick as thieves,
bent on stealing more freedom...
and we sure as hell did.

They said you didn't care,
but I have memories
that can't be touched
and Christmas cards
that say otherwise.

May you rest in peace,
you crazy motherfucker.

Help Me

With numb hands holding the chains,
and with watery eyes
obscuring my mental vision of you...
I'm not giving up.

You can't control it,
you fight it so much
you're losing sleep.

I'm tired of thinking,
tired of dreaming
about unresolved things.

Pain is as common
as the dissatisfaction
in one's own self.

If we have to suffer,
we want it to mean something,
and knowing that life isn't fair
doesn't exactly erase the thought
that this time could all be for naught...

I sincerely hope there's a reason
that leads to understanding—
if only for a little while.

In the meantime
help me to be a little better,
help me to take a little less,
and give a little more,

help me to not judge the world
or myself too harshly.

Help me clarify the purpose
and meaning to my life
so I can feel good about my actions...

dreaming myself free of the trap,
I am freedom
in all its forms,

the stillness and silence of peace,
and real love
for my friends
and family.

Today

There's a rising and falling,
a subtle ebb and flow of wind
and highway noise
that crashes like waves
on the back porch of a beautiful place in the country
not too far removed from the city.

Sunlight dances on oak leaves
and it also warms the cat
that sleeps at my feet.

The air is clean and cool
and it feels restorative—
as if you inhaled deeply enough
you might live another 100 years...
so I inhale
as much as my lungs can hold.

In this sublime stillness
there's relief
from the distractions
and the ongoing madness of the world,
and for a few precious moments
I know real freedom.

I don't always feel blessed,
but I do today.

True Love

It took my breath away
and breathed life back
into my tormented soul,

its incomparable light transformed me—
it was inside of me
the whole time
for all time.

It was rain falling
on a sunlit day,

my innocent child
rolling on the floor
playing with the dog,
shrieking with pure joy.

It was the plant
that hadn't bloomed in 20 years
that suddenly bloomed
after my Dad passed.

It was my Mom taking me in
when I had fallen
and spiraled out of control
and lost
what I considered to be everything.

It was the redemption in forgiveness
and the freedom in acceptance.

It was my brother and sister
showing up
when I needed them to.

It was smoking a cigar
with an elderly gentleman
who couldn't remember my name
as we listened to music
on the back porch.

It was isolation
on a beach
in the wintertime.

It was my heart
fastened to a kite
let loose on a mountain top,
sacrificed to the Santa Ana winds.

It was much more
than I ever imagined it to be.

It was releasing my parents' ashes
into the most beautiful rivers in Texas
with my siblings.

It was a game of cards
with my good friend
that started on Black Jack
and ended on Black Jack
for both of us...

Robert Knott

The Artist Inside

Another day,
another opportunity
to break free
and get away.

As you orchestrate your escape into freedom
and create something
that makes you proud,
something personal
that makes you forget yourself
as you start to sing loud,

and you no longer care
who can hear you,
and it's yourself
that you relax into,

you're not worried,
you're supposed to be happy,
you're supposed to have fun,

you have to let go
as you surrender control—
it's on you
if you're going to shine like the sun.

They're going to hate you
for whatever you do,
that's no surprise
and it's nothing new,

you remind yourself
that this is your one and only life,

so you breathe in
the things that make you feel good,
and you put a little paint
on your palette knife,

the one your sister gave you for Christmas—
and automatically
you feel your spirit lift.

You honor your life
by sharing
your greatest gifts.

Robert Knott

Infinite

Sacrifice...

your life for what's right
never dies,

a light that flourishes
in hope for a better day,

a divine kiss
that warms your heart,

the freedom to start over,
the courage to never stop
trying for forgiveness,

the strength to embrace the truth,
the love that gives the end
a new beginning,

the peace to settle our wars,
the star that blows up the night—

it's our right
to fight for something so beautiful
it makes you cry

a river so pure in belief,
a faith that flows
from the depths of our soul,

the energy that creates the universe—

without your love
nothing's real.

A... Like

Like a man
who's recently lost his vision
and is stumbling around in the dark

Like a man
who doesn't recognize
that he's hurting himself
and the ones he loves

Like a man
who has lost all patience
and wants to be left alone

Like a man
who can't ask for help
because his pride is too great

Like a man
who can't stop worrying
because he's not connected
to the present moment

Like a man
who is too quick to anger
and forgets himself

Like a man
who is not his own best friend
and is lashing out

Like a man
that lusts after power and control

And also...

Like a man
that lifts the wreckage off a stranger

Like a man
that thinks for himself
at the critical moment
and has integrity
and love in his heart and soul

Like a man
that knows his children
are watching him
to know what is right

Like a man
that just decides
that he's going to do better
every day in every way

Like a man
that embraces pain
and turns it into something beautiful
that helps people

Like a man
that remembers
the strongest forgive
and that freedom is found
in a state of love and acceptance
without judgment

Like a man
that knows he has more to give
and much more to learn

Like a man
who rebuilds cities
and preserves the sanctity of nature

What kind of men and women are we?
More alike than we realize.

Out the Ground

Deep inside your crazy heart,
getting lost in your unknown art,
it's up to you,
make the myths and wild dreams come true

They'll try to beat your hopes down,
keep 'em coming out the ground,
you laugh and smile at the pain,
you're a force of nature that's insane

They'll try and lock you up,
steal your freedom—
and for what?

Don't be a slave,
fight,
stay strong
and be brave!!!

Keep it coming out the ground,
show the world the beauty that you found,
it's your gift,
it's your life,
double down on yourself,
pay the price

Evolving Chaos

I don't know what to say,
I'm not sure that I can explain it
and make it ok.

I don't possess the grace
to put your mind at ease.

I'm waiting for something
that's not coming,
or maybe I'm just too blind to see it,
and maybe it's here,
and I'm too fucked up to realize it.

I don't know,
I want to know...

Tragedy lurks behind every tomorrow,
tears for sorrow
no one wants to feel.

I can see the chaos
but where's the harmony?
I can hear the music
but where's the joy?

Destruction, death, and disease—
that's all I hear about these days...

Global warming,
resources running out,
extinction on the rise,
Mother Nature's on the war path,
and humanity gets cleansed
in its own blood bath.

Greed, hunger, war, poverty, ignorance,
parasitic relationships
eating up creation.

Maybe it's too late to save ourselves,
maybe this is the way it's supposed to be...

Positive, negative,
nothing and everything,
love, hate,
light and darkness,
wrong, right,
blinded by sight,
hope, sorrow,
Heaven, Hell,
freedom, slavery
inside a cell.

I breathe in the air,
and I taste the pollution,
so many problems,
but where are the solutions?

Digital transformation,
pirated information,
prescriptions for the pain,
institutions for the insane,
acid for the rain,
guilt for the shame...

I'm in need of relief
but no one wants to give...

You have to die
for the life you want to live.

Robert Knott

The Cure

It's so good to see you,
I never want to say goodbye.

When I think of you
I can't help but smile,
remember how we'd laugh
till we'd break down and cry?

You were always there
living deep down inside,
my heart bleeds for you,
a river that's wild and free.

Love is what we've got—
it will always be.

There's no one
that could take your place,
you were always
one of a kind.

I could always be myself—
you gave me peace of mind.

You would really listen
to the things I had to say.
When things got too bad
you'd make me feel okay.

Your love is a light
that shines
for the universe to feel.

When I think of you,
there's a truth that's real.

We've got a bond
that time could never break.

You always gave me a hope
that sorrow
could never take.

The Return of Grace

May you see
with extraordinary eyes
beneath the surface of things

and smile in your heart
at the pain that wrecked,
addicted,
and transformed you,

as it wanes
like an ebbing tide

leaving freedom in its wake
to explore
good and beautiful things.

Nonlinear

Nonlinear
is the only way you're gonna get there.

One with the chaos,
I was thinking
and that was my first mistake.

There's no book
that substitutes
for your own experience.

They tell you not to feel,
and if you listen
it won't be real,
it will be contrived...

that's not how the spirit shines
but who knows?

I write from the gut,
and I'm throwing up.

It's a fine line
between discipline and freedom.

Trust what you feel,
not what you think...

that's easier said
than done.

Still Learning

Where to begin?
I'll start at the end.

No one gets by in this world
without help from someone.

There may come a day
when you no longer know what you're doing,
why you're here,
or even who you are...

How are you going to handle it?
How are you going to be okay
when you've lost your mind
or when your heart is broken?

It's when you've lost everything
that you understand what's truly important,
and yet it's hard to put yourself in that place
if things are going well.

I'm not sure what I'm trying to say—
only that if there's a truth to be uncovered,
I hope it reveals something that will help...
though in my experience,
the truth hurts
just as often as it heals.

To me,
there's this constant struggle
between light and dark matter
in all forms of energy
and planes of existence.

Human nature contradicts,
and emotion often defies logic and reason
no matter how hard you try
to keep a level head.

I've known of instances
where pain had to be embraced—
and also
where there was no way to endure it
and keep on living
without going completely insane.

The only option
was to escape it
by doing whatever it took,
and by any means necessary...
so that you could survive.

I've seen it turn into addiction and slavery—
and also create a discipline and fortitude
within oneself
that liberated the soul.

I've seen something I can't fully explain
go back and forth
over and over again
in countless ways,

illustrating a duality of experience
in a spectrum that's infinite and chaotic
where change is constant.

We all have these stories—
some are true,
others are make-believe,
and many are just varying depths and degrees
of our interpretations
of good and evil.

What's the point?
Maybe there isn't one...

The thing that destroys you
is the same thing that brings you back to life
in a different time.

I've lived at least half my life
and I want to understand,
even though I'm pretty sure
it ultimately won't do me much good.

"Free will"...what's it good for?
How often do we want
what we know isn't good for ourselves—
let alone somebody else?

What are the ultimate truths?
I know that I love
freedom,
joy,
peace,
art,
music,
my friends,
my family,
and people that have love in their hearts.

I'm learning
that if you want more,
you also have to give more...

Robert Knott

A Truth

It's both objective and subjective
and it's something beyond either one.

I have no words of wisdom
other than life will give you things you're not equipped to deal with,
and when that happens
it's going to take time,
it's going to take reflection,
it's going to take more than you ever thought you had to give.

And that's both beautiful and terrifying.

You can turn to God,
you can turn away,
and you'll still be here...
at least for a little while.

I'm thinking, to be yourself
is a noble worthwhile pursuit.

My ego says no one can do it better,
my true self says I can't do it without you.

It's a minor miracle
I'm not addicted to heroin
and shooting my life away...
even though I dream about it
more than I care to admit.

I love you...
and dream about you more.

The Shining Soldier

Battered, bruised, and broken...
he won't stay down,
so he keeps fighting,
pleasure in the pain at hand,
in time numbness takes over
but his heart won't let him surrender.

Self destruction enter sacrifice,
a lost soul hides,
guarded by shields of denial,
waiting for salvation
in an eternal war of the spirit.

Europa

Built me a little spaceship,
I'm leaving Earth behind,
I'm striking out for Europa,
got to find some peace of mind

I'm leaving this world
for a moon that's covered in ice,
I feel really cold now
so Europa might be nice

Europa, here I come,
your weather won't bother me
cause I'm already oh so numb

Fuck the bullshit,
fuck the bullshit

Flying fast now in outer space
going to Europa
where there's no one on my fucking case

When I get to Europa
gonna build me an igloo
then I'm gonna do
whatever the fuck it is that Europans do

Out in Europa
no one feels a thing,
everyone is blue out here
just like everything

Fuck the bullshit,
fuck the bullshit

Europa
a moon that's covered in ice,
when you feel cold inside
there's no place quite as nice

Europa
that's where ya want to go,
just ask any alien—
they already know

Europa
it's quite unique,
when ya want to disappear
and everything feels oh so bleak...

Europa, here I come

Reconstruction

That's what you do
when you've been devastated by hard times.

By any means necessary
you do whatever it takes
(*without hurting others or yourself*)
to get to where you need to be...

You stop doing the things
you used to do
to mask and kill the pain.

You get brutally honest with yourself
and find the will
to make the changes you need to make
so that you can have
a beautiful reality and existence.

You accept,
sacrifice,
trust,
forgive,
and respect who you are
by having faith in yourself

and try to make each day
as good as you can possibly make it
by living in the present.

Dimension

You live in so many worlds...
this makes me smile...

I sit in the corner of a dark room
smoking a blunt
with my feet kicked up,
it's far too late
and way too early,

the time slips
as it unfurls and unfolds...
seamless...
it blooms...
and it awakens my soul,
so I can no longer sleep.

I pick up my pen...
I write for the muse that is you,
and I write for the poet inside me,

the smoke from the plume
is something to behold and see...

I explore the corridors of a mind
that is at polar opposites
of a spectrum that is extreme.

I traverse the empty
yet full chambers
of a beating drum
that is my dialectic arrhythmic heart...

blindly...
I trip and I fall,
as I stumble forward,

with its secret doors
and its myriad of hues...

the depths,
and the mercurial degrees...

this love is an abyss
that is blissful
and so very deep...

a mixture of fire and ice...
the elements dance
in a cataclysm of chaotic space,
and a truth reigns supreme...

the light that is bright
is infinite...
ever so radiant...

it shines...
from eyes that are gray...
come forth
the seven infinite colors of the rainbow
and the peace
is yours
and mine...

Thank You

Thank you for my life...
the joy and the strife.

The pain I didn't understand...
helping me to become a better man.

The hate that was transformed
so love could transcend...
the ego silenced
so that the true self
could find its voice again.

I see the sun shining from inside of you...
it reminds me of what's beautiful and true.

Freedom is not being afraid...
letting go of everything
that negative emotions unconsciously made.

Music is created
with its healing power...
and there's relief
found in this sacred hour.

Christmas Day

Loss,
rebirth,
forgiveness for sins,
sunlight in the morning...
it's a bit overwhelming.

Shed a single tear
for the death of a friend,
and one more in happiness
for the beautiful son
that sleeps beside me.

The dog licks my hand,
then rests his head on my shoulder.

Son,
me,
dog...
our own sort of trinity.

A Wonderful Life
meets *Miracle on West 8th Street.*

And it feels
both impermanent
and eternal
at the same time.

I see myself on a beach,
and alone getting strong in the mountain,
exploring the depths,
ascending to new heights...

ubiquitous and esoteric,
lost and found
in my own reality.

The cold air,
the warmth of a good blanket,
and cognizant
of the precious time in space.

To be alive
and smiling
out of both gratitude
and determination.

The Trick

It's a trap,
the trick is to realize that there is no trap...
it's a mind fuck.

You think you're stuck
and you are...
you think yourself free
and the obstacles disappear.

It's not easy
because they want you in the trap,
so they bombard you
and over stimulate you
till you're too tired
to do anything about it.

If you want freedom
you have to disconnect from the culture,
the society that promotes fear,
obsession,
and a cure that doesn't exist.

You are the cure
for your pain,
for your predicament,
for your reality.

There's no prescription
that's going to get you free.

It's you
turning your back on the world
and experimenting
and exploring
what works best for you.

If you want to be free
you have to both forgive and forget
everything you were ever taught.

You have to separate yourself
from the self you've always known yourself to be.

I didn't say it would be easy
but I know how you get there.

You create a new format,
one that doesn't involve the pain you've experienced,
one that is new in the present moment.

One that doesn't succumb
to the identity
you've always known yourself to be...

you forget yourself...
and you smile
and sleep
like you did in the womb,
before the world had a chance to get at you...

you recreate yourself
before your Mom and Dad's inexperience
tainted your evolution,
or anyone else
who guided you away
from what was actually best for you.

You listen to your heartbeat
and breathe,
needing nothing
but the awareness
of a consciousness
born of your own spirit.

I'm not there yet
but I'd like to get there before I die
just to say
"fuck you
and I love you
but I'm going to be me
and that's enough."

The Responsibility of Awareness

A crisis or emergency
that consistently reappears every few weeks
is a pattern within a cycle
that should be broken
by the consciousness and awareness
of one's own behavior and choices.

It's not up to anyone else to save you,
you must save yourself
from your own past,
your own identity
that clings to your own painful experience.

Make no mistake...
man is in love with his pain
just as much
as he is in love with his pleasure.

If you truly, sincerely desire to be free
you must abandon your thoughts
and listen to the intelligence of your own heart
and free yourself
from your self.

Futility of Communication

It's the age of distraction
and sensory overload
where they simply can't hear you,

and even if they could
they're not ready to—
and that's not their fault.

Also,
people in pain,
they can't hear you either...

they're too wrapped up
in the thing that's making them suffer
so all their attention is on that...

you can't make somebody arrive somewhere
before they're sincerely
and genuinely ready—
it's just a fact.

So you're left
talking to yourself
because you're the only one
that understands
where you're at
and what you're going through.

What I Never Said...

I'm sorry...
I wasn't listening or feeling
because I was too wrapped up in myself...
in my own pain,
in my own experience.

I think you're beautiful.
I know you're beautiful.

This life is strange.
There's so much bullshit,
so much distraction,
so much...
almost too much.

A moment of clarity crashes
like a rogue wave...
things happen
and you find that you're not the same.

Life changes you
and you absorb what's meant for you.
You see and feel things
you never expected.
It hits you
when you least expect it.

People grow and heal at different rates
and if you're lucky
you find that person
that's in the same place
at the same time...

so in a sense
it's rare...
there is magic in the world.

The truth is meaningless without understanding...
you can't really tell people what you know
if they've never been there,
if they haven't sincerely arrived.

It's not their fault,
and it's not yours either...
it is what it is...

I've had more money
than I knew what to do with,
and I've been so broke
that I didn't know how I was going to survive...

and it was all in my mind.

Myth,
stories,
identity,
legend...
it's all creation
and destruction.

Perhaps that's how we're wired...
I don't know.

What I do know
is that it matters...
it exists.

You give
whatever you have to give.
You suffer
because you think it's unfair

until you're submerged
in something deeper than yourself.

When you see someone fighting to breathe,
someone fighting to stand up,
someone that's lost all their faculties...
it's ugly and beautiful
at the same time.

It's not wrong or right,
it's gray.

To escape yourself
is like breaking out of Alcatraz.

I've never slept better
than when I was imprisoned...
and I've never felt more alive
than when everything was on the line.

It's the simple things
that give way to genius.
It's the complications
that make for mastery.

What can I give?
What can I do
to give this life more meaning?

It's a gift—
all this pleasure and pain—
and if you look at it from outside yourself
you see
that it's a miracle.

Love
is the only meaning.

Blood absorbs light...
because life
is light.

It's not wrong or right...
it just is.

Robert Knott

Subconscious Algebra

Tumultuous flashbacks
and dreams of dysfunction...
am I destined to be haunted forever?

Slamming cabinets
and doors rattling in my sleep,
scenarios invented
to torment my brain.

Sometimes a thing happens
and you're powerless to avoid it—
you can make peace with it,
but you still have to carry it...

hold on
and be strong.

If you need help,
don't let your pride and ego
prevent the asking...

Walk with You

Open my heart
so I can receive
both your light and darkness,

I think now
is the time we've been waiting for...

and I have something to say too...

You asked me how I was doing...
I won't give you a generic answer like
"I'm okay."

I woke up one morning
after a night of intense self-destruction
and I just said
"fuck it"
and started smiling,

whatever happens
that's what's supposed to happen—
whether I think it's amazing or not.

I decided
I was just going to make the best of it
with whatever I had
wherever I was...

it doesn't really matter
unless it's truly life-threatening...
not comfort-threatening.

I started with silence,
and moved into stillness—
and it's a practice,

like all the things
that are hard
and also
make your life better.

Undefeated

Caught the perfect wave
in the midst of the perfect storm,

washed up on a beach
naked,
gasping for breath,
bloody,
and torn...

my only thought
was gratitude for having survived,

and I smiled
at the warmth of the sand
as the crashing waves
lapped at my feet...

I've lost many battles
but my love for life
is infinite
and knows no defeat.

Robert Knott

Return to You

Of the light
from whence you came...

shine simply
and beautifully...

son, daughter, brother, sister,
mother, father, true friend...

One.

Be the silence
in the stillness that you need
and know that there can only be
that which you are.

There is a humble rectitude
that lives inside us
not born for judgement
but to bear witness to a truth.

A truth that one must always return to...
the innocent, the pure, the unadulterated...
sunlight of being.

The pain you feel
must be transformed
and you must not fear the change
for it is natural, boundless, infinite,
creative, peaceful, and free...

so smile for no reason
is greater than your own
beautiful heart.

Big Bang

We were floating
in a sea of multicolored lights.

There was no fear or pain,
it was as if all our worldly wants,
needs, desires, and troubles
had suddenly disappeared.

I thought this must be Heaven—
for you were there
and I felt at peace
and at one
with every living thing.

It felt infinite...

Then I found myself alone,
writhing in agony,
a slave to desire and temptation
eating me from the inside out,

fear overwhelming me
and turning my soul black.

This also felt infinite.

It was as if time and space
had stretched my soul out
between light and darkness
in a war
between positive and negative energy.

I could feel myself slipping
in and out of consciousness

and wondering how I would
possibly continue to exist.

I was remembering
and simultaneously forgetting
multiple lifetimes
and alternate realities—
and I came to
unsure of my own name...

So when you see the man or woman
standing quietly alone
with their arms crossed and folded,
and looking standoffish...

if you look closer
it could be that they're really
just trying to hold themselves together.

Big Bang
taking place in the core of their being,
and they may be wondering
if anything is going to be left
when it's all said and done—
and what was the meaning.

And if they happen to smile
and shed a tear,
then it might be
that they realized
what some of you
have already discovered
and know
at the deepest level.

That love was the meaning—
and it's a truth
that's beautiful,

ugly,
and impossible to describe,

for it is infinite
and responsible
for the birth and death
of our greatest joy and pain.

It is undefinable
and beyond comprehension.

And if you love them—
or even if you don't—
you may want to do them
a small kindness
and remind them
of who they are...

The Child

We pour over you,
the gentle warm water that bathes you,
and cleanses us,
and we are soaked
in the great fortune that is you.

We tend the beautiful
untainted gardens
of your innocent and voracious mind,
and our spirits grow
with fertile love.

We sing,
dance,
change our voices,
we do anything and everything
to see you smile—
and when you laugh
we are the happy fools for you.

We fly through the house
with you and to you,
pop wheelies in your stroller,
and are surprised when you fall asleep—
and when you awake
we are excited
even in our exhaustion.

We thought we knew what love was,
and then you made us think and feel again,
and it made us better,
and it made us stronger.

We hold you
and know how a blessing feels,

when you cry
or shriek with joyful glee,
and we are amazed
and inspired.

We begin to understand
what we never considered,
and we know
that we have to fight for change that's good,
and we are reborn
ready
and renewed.

We are learning
that we have more to learn,
and being taught
just as much as we teach,
and remembering
that there is something new
that's good
is possible
every day.

Passing Thoughts

Give me the gristle...
something that I can chew on
and ultimately get nothing from,
cause nothing is what it's all about.

I think all you can do
is try to operate from a place of peace and calm,
hopefully in a state of love without judgment.

All you have and all you are is right now,
it's not reliving the past
or worrying over the future.

You should do what you think is best for yourself
because only when you're at peace
can you give it to anybody else.

Accepting yourself as you are
and as the world and God made you
is probably one of the more difficult things to do in life...
you have all these judgments
and comparisons to let go and ignore...

the truth is
we're all ugly,
beautiful,
less than great,
and amazing.

If you want immediate peace,
stop thinking about what you don't have
and help somebody that is suffering
or in need of help.

It's not cool to be indifferent
when half your life is over...
it's cool to give a fuck.

And at the same time,
if it compromises your energy
and doesn't add value to your life,
you also need to not give a fuck...
relatively speaking.

Teach me a lesson I'll never learn...
I'll have won, lost,
and broke even some other way.

When you lose track of time
doing something that you love
and it's not destructive...
that's a clue you should be doing that thing more often.

Too much is the same as not enough...
let go,
accept,
and smile at the adversity
and absurdity.

If you died today,
is what you're carrying
something you want to take into the next life?

It's completely possible
that your life is playing out
in a myriad of infinite ways
in other dimensions.

So you might want to lay that burden
or grudge down.

A person's mind
is the source of their freedom
and enslavement.

Your thoughts
give rise to your feelings,
and your feelings
are the reason you behave
and act a certain way...

so if you have anxiety,
that usually stems from
attaching too much meaning
or weight
to your thoughts.

Give yourself a break,
and you'll give everyone else a break
that's around you.

If this is a simulation
and we're all the imagination of ourselves,
then I'm praying for a better imagination
in this lifetime.

How can they know you,
when they don't know themselves?

Experience is unique to the individual...
separate,
united...

I would venture to say
most everyone is searching for meaning
and understanding.

I know that I don't know
so maybe that's something.

It takes sincere desire
to arrive at any kind of real understanding.

Questions with No Answers

I'm tired of the world sometimes...
I think death would be easier.

Unfortunately or fortunately
I'm a warrior.

I still have something to give,
I still have love to convey,
I still have time
to change my perspective.

I won't tell you how I've suffered.
I'll only tell you
that I'm not done.

And perhaps I never will be...
I am
despite not understanding "why"...
I am
for what it's worth,

and I don't think it's for
what society tells me it is...

There was a man
who didn't like his thoughts and feelings
so he rearranged them with a shotgun.

It left the ones
he claimed to love
with a real sense of confusion
that was already there...

Robert Knott

Reprieve

Take flight from your misery,
let go of the mind
and its incessant calculations.

Life is passing you by
while you're stuck in deliberation with the self,
counting positives and negatives...
and none of it matters—
or at least not for long.

I've seen 18 year olds that were 80
and vice versa,
which one are you?

There's no wrong answer.

Are you living your life,
or the one someone else mapped out for you?

Time is more valuable than money,
by a long ways,
and if one hasn't figured that out,
one will probably never figure that out.

I only know
what I feel in my heart.

That you feel love
when you need it
at that most desperate hour—
that is my prayer.

There's no black and white now,
only gray.

Let's Be Real

Life is a choice and a gift.
You can fear and hate
or you can love and uplift.

You can bemoan your circumstance
or you can smile
and break out into your own unique kind of weird little dance.

You can see it as both a miracle and a curse
where you can't take it anymore
or you sigh and say
"it could always be worse."

It's true it can be cruel and unfair,
it can also be incredibly beautiful,
mysterious,
and rare.

For some of us it's a roller coaster—
there are days when you're thrilled beyond words,
laughing and enjoying the ride,

and then there are others
where you're throwing up
wondering how you're going to survive.

You can stress yourself to death
with worry over what you can't control,
or you can accept and let go
as you try and relax
into the most beautiful version
of your own soul.

You can be the judge,
the jury,
and the executioner,

or you could simply choose
to be kind,
merciful,
and forgive
whatever transgressions there were.

You can take what you want,
or give what they need—
it's a matter of selfishness or selflessness,
to heal someone or make them bleed.

You can stay in your own way,
or resolve to help someone
for no reason other than it's today.

You could choose to radiate something good that's pure,
or you could subjugate the world
like some kind of bullshit fuhrer.

You could always kill yourself
and take the easy way out,
or you could turn to prayer
so that your love and faith
is stronger than the fear and doubt.

Or maybe you're a man or woman of science
and in need of real proof—
the truth is
you don't have to believe in God
to be a good human
who's thankful for another day,
drinkable water,
clothes,
and a roof.

You can trust your instincts
and follow your own heart,
or you can play it safe
and settle on a role
that's less than who you really are
and not an original part.

I've heard it said
that blame is a wonderful thing—
for it absolves you from responsibility
so that you're the one
that doesn't have to make a change.

All I know
is that I don't really know,
but I'd be willing to bet
that love is the real purpose
of this strange, deadly, and beautiful game.

And though we may look and be very different
we're also very much the same.

You can live in denial
or pretend that it's not true,
but if people remember anything,
it's what you gave
and how you made them feel
when they were broken,
lost,
and didn't know what to do.

You can lose yourself to ego
and your own foolish pride,
you can also find
and represent your true self
when you can no longer run or hide.

You can be the cure
or you can be the disease,
you can be rude as fuck,
or you can say "thank you" and "please."

No matter what we say,
it's what we do—
we can unlearn and reprogram
what no longer serves,
or we can stay on the same old path
that leads to nothing new.

Hopefully we can agree
to leave this world better than we found it
and maybe shine a little grace,

but let's be real...

life is a choice and a gift
and it's on us
if we take it for granted
or if we rise up
to honor this truly magnificent time and place.

I Remember You

The madness and the laughter...
it lives inside me,
more than maybe
I ever wanted it to.

Songs come on the radio
and I can hear you singing.

Some things hurt you
and make you strong
at the same time.

I'm still learning,
still fucking up,
still as a dead calm
in a forgotten ocean
and still as tumultuous
as a Texas thunderstorm.

I miss you
so much more
than I ever thought I would...

you were a contradiction
that defied explanation.

Singular

Flying high
over walls built by hate and fear,
forgiveness is the gift I gave myself
so I'm in the clear,

music comes to life
as joy and pain
reverberate inside rain
that falls on a sunlit day,

a singular truth
blurred and misunderstood
as I sail and trip
looking for a better way,

laughing at the horror
'cause I don't know what else to do,
drinking and smiling to myself
as I pour a little liquor out
and think of you,

you're always here
no matter how hard
or lonely things get,

clinking glasses with ghosts
and great friends
celebrating times
that are impossible to forget,

we're making history
in the here and now,
living for the moment
'cause we're still alive somehow...

isn't it amazing?

Robert Knott

Crack in the Mirror

It's the crack in the mirror,
an imperfect reflection
that can't be any clearer

Watch me break free,
then lock myself up indefinitely

I'm a contradiction,
somewhere between truth and fiction

A cautionary tale
that's priceless
and cheap as fuck,
all I know is nothing
and that's too much

I'm the fire that burns
deep in your heart,
and then I'm the faith you lost
when everything fell apart

I want you to understand
but I don't want to explain,
I'm the confusion
that's fundamental
and drives you insane

I don't know what day it is
but I always know the time,
I'm a guilty prisoner
that's innocent of the crime

I've got a message
that's broken and distorted,
but it's crucial

that it gets delivered
and recorded

There's no in between,
just a whisper and a shout,
I feel fucking crazy
but I love what it's about

It's the promise of a new day
and the likely oncoming
of some world disaster,

and it's another impossible situation
that has you scratching your head
that brings about the laughter...

it's a complicated life
simplified by real love.

You're Not Like Me

"You're not like me,"
said the dragonfly to the bee.

"You've got little wings and funny stripes,
I don't think we can be friends,
we're not the same types."

"That's true, we're really different," said the bee,
"but we both belong to the insect family.

I think we should kick it,
I'll buzz and you hum,
we've got this whole lake and thicket—
it might be fun."

"I don't know,"
said the dragonfly to the bee,
"this could end up a catastrophe."

"Yes, that's true," said the bee,
"but I'd rather have you as a friend
than an enemy."

The dragonfly was taken aback,
he had never really thought of it like that...

Some birds and fish
had eaten up all his good friends—

it might be a little strange at first,
but it very well
could be win/win.

The Real You

Is relaxed
and quietly smiling
from the inside out,
you are at peace.

There are no judgments
or comparisons
that hinder your experience
or your perspective.

You are at one
with yourself.

You know you're not perfect
but you are in pursuit of excellence.

You don't need validation,
you don't need recognition
or accolades.

All you need
is love for yourself and others
and a willingness to help
and to be of service.

It's not about religious
or political beliefs,
it's about living a life
that makes you feel good
about who you are
and what you do...

It's about emotional balance
and spiritual growth.

It's about helping a stranger
that can do nothing for you.

It's about being better than yesterday
but also forgiving yourself
when you're not.

It's about trying again
even though you feel paralyzed
and you're terrified.

It's about accepting
what you can't change
and letting go
of what no longer serves you
in the pursuit of your best life.

It's actions and words
in alignment.

It's about empathy
and putting yourself
in someone else's shoes,
and then walking
till you understand
that they're not so different from you.

It's gratitude
and mindfulness
and a meditative state,

and it all coalesces
out of love.

Infinite Expressions

Our world's are entwined
Our spirit's pour out love
Our minds break free
from the pressure of gravity...

Tomorrow is the past
and the present is woven
in between the dimensional threads of reality,

to see the truth before it is known,
to know something you can't explain,
to behold the miracle as it occurs
and do justice to the meaning,

to understand what doesn't make sense,
to feel the presence
of something greater than yourself,

to live inside and outside
the realms of experience
as you look into and throughout
the parallels of time and space,

to dive into and rise above what you are
as you transcend from nothing into everything
over and over again,

to the end in its beginning,
created from a belief that it matters...

a star shatters into infinite expressions
and the universe lives
in its sacrifice.

Vast Expanse

The fire
that can never be extinguished,

the love
that will never be relinquished,

the father of the son,
the son of the father,
the bond...

past,
present,
future,
and beyond,

life through death,
into the abyss of nothingness,
where space and time
cease to exist...

the ghost of a particle strikes,
then strikes again,
something less than an atom sparks,

the smallest of flames flicker,
and an ember burns
seven infinite colors
then radiates,

the energy is immense,
it gets condensed
beyond science,

and returns
as love explodes

in matter
that is both light
and dark...

love never needed a reason...
all it ever needed
was a spark.

Aren't We All

Digging for fire...
through the inexplicable muck of our lives
and the inevitable mire.

Hurdle after hurdle,
pitfall after pitfall,
gasping for breath
and wondering
how we're going to find
the wherewithal...

to keep going,
to keep growing,
to keep flowing
in the best way possible
towards who we are
and why we're here...

I don't know what they're doing
so I'm just going to do my own thing
and keep trying
to find a better way.

Robert Knott

Universe to Love

Lee Morgan in the depths of absolution,
feels like a junkie getting high on *Revolución*

Playing catch with my dog
while puffin on a cigar,
contemplating progress
and just how far

Greasy cheeseburger
with jalapeños and a Mexican coke,
it hurt but I laughed it off
like it was a joke

Killer bass line
infecting me with the sound,
hunting the subjective and objective truth
like a starving bloodhound

Embracing the pain
that destroyed who I thought I was,
knowing that there was no reason for it,
accepting it just because

Alone in a crowded room
unable to escape isolation,
giving more of my soul for free
not expecting any material thing or compensation

Recognizing
that I need to put my ego in check
before it cancels out what's right,
getting back up and giving more
even though I've tired of the fight

Hoping that I can live up to these words
and not be overwhelmed by feeling,
reminding myself
that there's no limit and no ceiling

Asking for forgiveness
that I'm not sure I want or deserve,
hitting it out the park
the next time life throws me a curve

Breaking free of labels, status quos,
and all other forms of constraint,
channeling something supernatural
and smiling
right before I feint

Reading and listening more
out of respect for others' experience
yet not discounting my own,
knowing there's karma
for which I still need to atone

Waking up to the fact
that my judgment and expectations
are foolish pride,
having faith that I can do better
as long as I keep mining
what's inside

Emergent

Merge into the music,
disappear into the art,
write from the soul,
find your bliss—

and it won't matter
if the world falls apart...

for you'll be creating something new,
and the world needs
the imaginations of men and women
bent upon improving the world
for the sake of each other.

My Friends the Four Winds

When I was lost
and didn't know what to do,
I could always count on you...

When I was in trouble
and about to go insane,
you showed up like a hurricane
destroying the hopelessness
I felt deep down in the earth,

it was like
a miraculous kind
of spiritual rebirth...

When I needed clarity of mind
I felt the wind blow from the East...

When I needed the truth pointed out
I felt the wind blow from the North...

When I needed a safe place
to rest my head
I felt the wind blow from the West...

And when I needed to be encouraged
I felt the wind blow from the South.

I know
without the four winds
I would never have gotten
anywhere at all.

The Presence of One

Silence is your best friend.
Words are meaningless
unless born with the intention of love.

Actions are telling.
Your essence stands still.
You emanate joy
despite the interpretation of pain.

You smile at the disrespect
because you know
it can only touch you
if you allow it.

You accept and let go,
you remember and you forget,
you know the only thing that matters
is the presence
of the one you are
eternally
right now.

You laugh,
you feel the seriousness
in your arrival,
and know the solution
through the intelligence of the heart.

Your world belongs to you
and there's even more there
when you give it away.

The dissolution of self
is a victory for the soul
and it benefits everyone.

You feel the lightness
of a being that shines,
as you radiate life.

You are the color,
you are the music,
you are the meaning
that reveals the purpose...

anything and everything...
it's the oneness
that exists
behind the illusion
of separation.

Fishing

Laying in my bed,
swimming in my head,
thinking about the birth and destruction.

How the energy and the darkness
play upon one another
and how color came to light.

How an image of somebody you love
gets burned into your mind,
and tears of joy and pain
flood the soul.

Searching the world over
as you fall inside yourself
and rise out of the ashes
of your own burning heart.

They say they understand
but no one does...

I'm almost to the point
where I no longer care
what anyone thinks about me
and I'm running faster towards it,

I'm only interested in living
and being free.

Knowing I'm in jail
with the key in my pocket
this whole time...

the crimes we commit against our self
are the same ones
we commit against everyone else.

That's why we hate them—
because they're a reminder
that we're no better.

People hate the truth
they're not ready to hear,
it's scary
to step outside a delusion
created to avoid fear and pain.

When love hurt you the most
it was a self-created survival mechanism
that hardened your heart
as you raised the gates
and fortified your defenses—

and that allowed you to escape the feeling...
prolonging your sentence.

Unfortunately,
embracing the pain
and accepting the beautiful
and disfiguring truth
is your only chance
for redemption and liberty...

don't ask me how I know.

To Be

To be alive and still drawing breath with hope in your heart

To be truly grateful and thankful despite things falling apart

To be a peaceful warrior in the life long fight against yourself

To be kind, patient, and loving with the world for the sake of its health

To be alone in silence and content with that place in time

To be awake and still curious about the beauty you have yet to find

To be vigilant in keeping hate from your heart and negativity from your thoughts

To be able to laugh at the mistakes you've made and all the trouble you bought

To be suspended in time for a glorious precious moment

To be free in your body, heart, mind, and soul because you own it

To be in rhythm and in the zone playing or working like there's no tomorrow

To be reminded that there is more love on the other side of sorrow

To be on the verge of your very best and then going beyond that

To be true to yourself no matter what or where you're at

To be there in that place in time giving what you could

To be listened to and feeling like you were finally understood

To be one with great spirit because it's there inside you

To be the change you want to see because it's right and it's time to

To be and do your best and not give up even should more tragedy befall you

To be resilient and brave in the face of overwhelming odds and continue

To be the water in the desert that brings beautiful things back to life

To be the one that doesn't seek revenge, that holsters the gun, and puts away the knife

To be in love again, with the world, yourself, and with someone

To be seeking to share the beauty in this world and discovering the power of one

Breathe

Inhalation... clean blue sky
Exhalation... deep relaxing sigh
In various states of fear, stress, and confusion
A little girl with gray hair prays for grace and mercy and for her dying
father's absolution
Heaven holds a sense of recognition when
his hand falls and he breathes his
last breath
A sad smile as she kisses his forehead one last time, tears fall, not
wanting to accept her loss and his death
She can feel it now, life pulses, her heart is letting her know, it beats
like a drum pounding in her chest
Empathy wakes up in a vicarious field full of wild flowers and it's like a
time lapse, you see the cycle, the simple beauty of nature, and you take
some rest
Sunlight warms our faces and we're left to make peace with these voids
and all these spaces, the fabric is torn and there's nothing we can do
There's a dream of dimensional threads, and an instrument to weave
time back together just for a precious few
Sometimes it feels like all the world has gone dark, and it's underwater
collectively gasping for breath and writhing to get free
And I can't help but wonder about these things we have no control of,
so I'm praying and contemplating silently

Robert Knott

Sometimes

Sometimes I wonder if this is all an experiment gone wrong.

How can all these people that I love have died and gone?

It doesn't seem fair, so I take a long walk and it's my perspective and my heart in need of repair.

I force myself to smile, by any means I do whatever it takes...

I run another mile, have another drink, let myself be distracted, pray, work, play, and swim in rivers and lakes

And it sometimes helps but it also still hurts so I try to both accept and let go of the pain

And it sometimes feels like I've become addicted to it or that I've gone insane

So I laugh at the wrong things or at inappropriate times, drop random tears, and talk to myself while I drive

I remind myself of life's many blessings and to be grateful for I loved them and they loved me and I know somehow inside me that they are still alive...

Sometimes I think of all the things I never got to say or do

And sometimes I'm angry, and sometimes I feel cheated, and sometimes it feels like I'll never heal and I'll be forever blue

Sometimes....

And then sometimes I find myself in a state of grace and completely aware of the love and light that fills up the heart and soul as it expands the space.

And sometimes I can still hear and feel them in the elements of nature as the sun shines and the rain falls, simultaneously on my face...

And sometimes like right now I find myself smiling and feeling joy and sorrow at the same time.

Sometimes...I realize it has to be this way.

The Highway Fiend

Let me tell ya, it was spooky boy!! It was a dark, dark scene...scarier than any Halloween. See I was traveling down the road late one moon filled night, when I come across a horrible sight. It was a ferocious beast to say the least, and he was looking at me like a Thanksgiving feast. He had razor sharp teeth and blood in his eyes, and then he let out a terrible cry. It was straight from hell as far as I could tell and I'd be lying if I said I wasn't scared, but I told that demon to make a move if he dared....see I'd always been quick with a gun the way lightning flashes, and even though that beast was frightening I felt I had a chance...so I smiled and asked that fiend if he cared to dance. Well he spit at me and howled at the moon and I could see he was thinking bout eating soon. So I pulled my pistol in the blink of an eye, and I said "if ya come any closer you're bound to die, I've got 6 silver bullets aimed at your heart and if you're lucky they might not blow ya apart." Well he could tell I was a mean son of a bitch and my trigger finger was a starting to itch. Now I could see that beast was having second thoughts bout the trouble he'd bought, but he was a bloody thirsty fiend with a desire to kill, and he wasn't leaving till he had his fill. So he started towards me and the bullets flew, my gun spoke loud and my aim was true. Well that demon lay there dying as day started to break and then I saw something I couldn't quite take. As the morning light fell on that hellish beast I saw him change back into a man I once knew, and then he smiled and with his last breath said "thank you." Well now I'd never of believed it had I not seen it with my own eyes, and if I were you I might think it was a pack of lies...but if you're ever traveling down the road late on a moon filled night...beware of the highway fiend and his damnable plight.

Reflections

Inside a wax museum of freaks, villains, and heroes, reflected in a house of mirrors, into the haunted house, twisted inside out, riding a merry-go-round, defying death's gravity and knowing no bounds, in a ring of fire the lion tamer laughs at ferocity, in the big house where the elephant runs from the mouse.

Open to the Eternal

Some people you really love
and you have to let them go,
I think that hurts the most.

Your life isn't the same without them...
it's hard.

We don't talk about it
cause it can be depressing
and that's not what you want to project.

It's painful
but that's what life is—
it's taking that pain
and transforming it
into something that's focused
on love and growth.

I still feel the gravity of the void
no matter how much time passes.

You can't live life
and not experience loss.

You force yourself to smile
and carry on,
you don't know how you're going to manage,
you just do.

It's not pretty
and in reality
it's not very graceful.

They're in the best part of your heart,
so in that respect

they're always with you—
but it's not the same.

Real love is forever...
love isn't a feeling,
it's an ability.

So whether you're still in my life or not,
I still have major love for you
and I will hold it,
just in a different way...

in a way that frees me,
and I hope you know
that your smile
is burned into my heart.

Minnie Faye

She was a strong West Texas gal

with a great big fiery gentle heart

My friend, my pal

It hasn't hit me yet but I know it will

There'll be one more hole I can't fill

And that's okay that's just the way it goes

But I'm lucky and blessed for having known you and there's a river of love that forever flows

She was a strong West Texas gal

With a great big fiery gentle heart

My friend, my pal

Lover of music, laughter, and winds that sail

You won't be forgotten even should my memory fail cause you're there in the best part of my heart that's grateful and true and there's a permanent warm feeling that reminds me of you

My strong West Texas gal.

All This Space and Time

Wild like the Yangtze
Deep like the Mariana
Mysterious like a jungle
shrouded in mist and moonlight...

Strong and free
like the hope that beats just for you...

No end
No beginning
Alive in dream
Beyond limitation

Lost and full of helium
Brave and boundless
You smile
Time breaks

Joy and pain reverberates
inside rain that falls infinite
on a sunlit day...

Primordial magic
Elemental and prime
Magnetic and strange

Lost in paradise
and regained in hell,
spit out and found
washed up
on a deserted beach...

Together and apart
Wrong and right
Forever

Parallel
and in another dimension
flying and falling into...

Us.

Missing in Action

There's a homeless man
waving an American flag,
he's a veteran
who's down on his luck,

there's a hopeless desperation
in his bloodshot eyes
that says what most of us
already think—

this guy's fucked up
and he just wants another drink.

He looks like a man
that needs some change,
he's disoriented
and he may never be the same.

He's still fighting a war,
it's just a different kind.

The windows roll up,
and the doors lock,
the people look away
'cause it's easier to ignore.

The Meta Culture

Upgrade to the happier version of yourself.
For only a few more personal freedoms
you can have it all.

We can numb you the fuck out
and bombard you
with more absolutely useless information and stimuli.

You too can be a product of a product,
a consumer
that's fully been consumed.

In the name of distraction
we'll help you to forget this reality,
and you can be the test subject
in our fucked up experiment
in whatever the fuck is going on,
or whatever you want to call it...

let's just do it!!

We can understand
and suffer the consequences later
at a more convenient time.

Not keeping up with the status quo?

By the time you realize what's happening
we will have melted your mind
and you can pay us
to give you better thoughts
that benefit our fucked up systems.

You won't have to think at all!!

Robert Knott

Black Swan

Swan dive
into a deep abyss.

Wake up on the other side
in a state of bliss.

There's no fear here
only strength and peace.

You've leveled up your own consciousness
in another dimension
where you have transcended
the entrances and exits.

It's always been here
waiting for you
to acknowledge
your own infinite presence.

The gift of existence
is underneath the form
and it's eternal,
like a flame that burns
outside of time.

Energy doesn't lie,
love is the reason
and light is the truth.

You understand
the pain you feel
is tied to the joy—
opposite ends of the same spectrum,
and one without the other
would be unnatural.

Man and his myths,
so concerned
with destruction and creation,
when it's the energy,
frequency,
and the vibration
that should be acknowledged
and celebrated.

Forget yourself,
dance motherfucker,
there are no systems of control here.

This is the dream within the dream
that's more real than the matrix.

This is how universes get created.
This is how gravity gets circumvented.

Beauty has no boundaries.
Freedom has no limits.
And space
is the only thing
moving faster than light.

And love,
in all its expressions,
the only real cure.

Robert Knott

Untitled

My heart is strong,
my love is deep
I've lost many times
what I've desired to keep

Accepting, letting go...
it's a river that's wild,
uncompromising,
as it crashes over a man-sized rock
with relentless flow.

Making peace
with what I'll never understand,
and explanations I'll never get,

Remember who you are, they say—
how easily I forget.

To have reverence
for an infinite moment,
and witness the divine,

it's what I'm here for,
as I give myself
the freedom
and the self love
to shine.

Reverence

For the songs of birds in the early morning

For the thunder and cleansing rain when it's storming

For the innocent child as they play and laugh with unbridled joy

For that furry friend whether it be a girl or a boy

For that real friend that sticks by you through thick and thin

For changing perspectives that help you to see things differently again and again

For unconventional thinking that's done outside the box

For the simple pleasure and ability to kick a rock

For the past, present, and future hard and soft feelings

For unlimited imagination and belief that helps you with growth and healing

For the new opportunity behind doors that were once previously locked

For the music that lifts your spirits and makes you feel like you can't be stopped

For the desire to improve and find a better way

For another chance to get it right and make the most of the day

For both the good and hard times that made you who you are

For the light that travels through vast darkness to illuminate no matter how far

For the warrior that fights on and on and doesn't give up

For the honor and experience of both loss and victory as we raise the cup

For the strength to continue when all hope seems lost

For the sacrifice and respect found in non material things that are both the value and the cost

For the peace and recovery beyond the sickness and all forms of pain

For the acceptance and forgiveness of things that will never be explained

For the present moment that's a gift and filled with real love

For the faith that's stronger than fear and the trust in God above

A Silver Heart

My words are ablaze—
I have to write my truest feelings
in the night sky
'cause my pen strikes sparks
and eats up the page.

My deepest thoughts
spread like a wildfire
pushed by hurricane winds,
rescuing the hopelessly lost
and disenchanted, when the
painful hell descends.

It's the beautiful truth
found in a fleeting moment
that's real
and right—
suspended forever
in the early morning's sweet light.

They bring warmth
to a world
that can be cruel and cold.

They're not for sale—
can't be bought
or sold.

They come from a lonely, empty place
forged by tragedy
and surreal pain—
free in my heart
made of silver,
not gold.

And the fire
rages
out
of
control
again.

It's everything that matters,
and nothing of consequence.

My pen—
the gladiator in the arena,
the convicted felon
longing for freedom
beyond the barbed wire fence.

It's my favorite weapon,
my faithful friend,
a force of nature
that
picks
up
the
wind.

Victory

I can't lose—
I refuse.

I've taken losses,
to be sure,
but as long as I breathe
I am not
ultimately
defeated.

I'll keep learning from my mistakes
and stay true
to who I know myself to be.

I will help where I can,
when I can—
because that's the kind of man
my parents raised.

And when I lose,
I'll be gracious in that defeat,
but I will still progress.

I'll keep working toward excellence.
I'll keep sacrificing
for what I know is right.

I'll rise toward the best of my spirit,
and before I die,
I will have achieved that—
not to impress,
not for applause—
but for the sake of my soul,
and the deep gratitude
I have for my own existence.

I will have fought my demons
to a standstill
and silenced them.

And my light
will shine
in its victory.

Every day is a blessing.
And I will continue
to give thanks—
no matter what
this life throws at me.

I will remember
and honor
the words of my father:

**"You are great.
Don't give up."**

And I haven't.

And I won't.

Alive

I live in the belly of an eagle

I am the scream before victory

I dive deep and rise high and feel the thrilling elation

I see far and wide as I soar through the clouds, my shadow falls across

the face of majestic peaks and beautiful valleys

I am of this earth and I am wild and free

The Catalyst

It was a trip to Mexico when I was super depressed. Thank you for driving.

There was a time when I was losing everything and you called and it turned into "how can I help"...and you gave them something better than I could and I was eternally grateful.

Alone in the quiet light drinking my anxiety away, knowing there's a better way.

Running around searching for you, and you're nowhere to be found.

There was you with that laugh and the dark sense of humor that almost always made me smile...it helped me to keep going.

I don't understand these tears or this insane laughter...perhaps I don't really know myself.

Coming Up

It almost seems like a fairytale with real monsters....I'm a survivor beyond what you could imagine. Not that you lack imagination but you weren't there, and for that reason you can't fully understand. I had it all and I also had it stripped. That's life, sometimes you get a reality that you're not equipped to deal with, so you adapt on the fly, you fail, you get back up, and you try then try some more. You ask God why this is what had to happen. You're emotionally exhausted, you psyche yourself up, cause that's what was instilled, you refill your cup. You pour it out, it disappears through the cracks as it disperses and absorbs into whatever it's meant for hopefully somehow transmuting into your dreams of something better. Would they dare to know? How you could feel so low and still have it so good? I get tired of talking about loss cause in this world it's an eventual reality and if you don't feel it now you'll feel it later. I'd rather talk about what made you feel free, and why that's not an everyday thing. It seems like it should be, like we should come to an understanding as to why joy is just an occasional experience.

Strong Wind of Change

From euphoric bliss to suicidal ideation to peaceful waves that turn tidal and destroy and revitalize creation you are, you are

Delirious as hell...I can't complain, raw I must maintain, knowing that it's mine to carry, fuck!!! it's mine to carry

Quotes and clichés don't fit nicely in the box, sometimes all you can do is laugh at your bruises and curse your hard knocks...you turn off the phone cause you need to be alone and isolation is an island unto yourself that you can control, and it's a quiet beauty, yes, it's quite beautiful, this deprivation you feel makes for fullness in time, it just takes so much time and there's no reason or rhyme and you lose and you find, yes, you lose and you find, that's what's cracked is still whole...and after all that's transpired, from being super low to high wired, the fact that you're still here is a miracle in itself, and faith is forever and always exactly what you have made it...and somehow, against all odds, you feel grateful...

For the ones cast down, the ones forgotten who survived the neglect, the ones who raised their own spirits with forgiveness, love and respect...the strong wind of change is for you.

Another Red Dawn

As the twilight of morning approaches, blood red horizons wash into another red dawn, leaving me transfixed by the sheer beauty of a world turning over. And as the most beautiful light crashes over a shining sea, somehow everything that was wrong disappeared inside of me...and I feel the strength restored in a faith that had been weakened.

Trade the Pain

Surfs up in the city...

Feel the heart of it, be a part of it, paddle out and drop in, get in the zone, make it your own, one with a crashing wave as the chains break for a modern slave, freedom, art, music, a force of nature, it's your own symphony...choose it. Trade the pain for euphoria, and have a drink on me.

My True Self

I sometimes feel overwhelmed by emotion, as if a valve broke inside me that day a long time ago, or maybe it's genetic, or just the way God made me, I don't really know. Today, I'm mindful that it can and often will supersede reason and logic. I perceive it as both a blessing and a curse. I have always been told I was too sensitive, too emotional. I don't like labels or classifications, or things that limit a person. Most of us limit ourselves without needing any help from anybody else, myself included. We choose to suffer a lot of the time for no other reason than to feel something real in a world that can seem fake and superficial. My true self isn't a victim, a pawn, an excuse, a stepping stone, or anything designed to be used or abused. My true self is here to help, heal, to be of service, to create, build, forgive, accept, detach, commit, respect, sacrifice, transform, transcend, and grow. My true self embraces struggle and pain and turns it into joy and triumph, it recognizes my own hate and transforms it into love that lights up the darkness. I'm a perfectly flawed human being and no better or worse than anyone else despite what my ego or shadow says...the truth is my light is greater than any darkness that tries to expand or creep in as long as I love myself and stay vigilant. For a long time I searched for a way out, the guilt and shame I felt deep down was sinking me and I was tired of living. I had lost almost everything that mattered to me at one point, there were drugs, then suicide (Dad), a miscarriage, death of a good friend (drugs), divorce, death of my oldest best friend (drugs) and then losing my Mom to cancer. The birth of my son saved my life, it gave me purpose, and I was able to start seeing the world with new eyes again. I doubt I'd still be here if it weren't for the birth of my son. For a while there it felt like I needed more love than anyone could give, now it feels like I have more love to give, so that's what this collection of poems, thoughts, writings, is about... love and growth. I'm not some self-help guru, just an artist, and a writer, who is attempting to make sense of the chaos and hopefully prevent someone from suffering more than they have to...silence is golden, and the only way out is in... thank you.

Sincerely,

Rob

Afterword

There was no purpose for this book other than me attempting to process many difficult emotions in relationship to the trials and tribulations of life. Hopefully it gives the reader something real that's useful in their own experience or journey. It was also simply about self expression, and living a life of creativity rather than one defined by loss and destruction.

I chose Robert Boyd Knott as a pseudonym out of love and respect for my Mom, her maiden name was Knott. She was a really good writer, and she burned her life's work up in a fire of her own making, so this is a way of honoring her, and a nod to her as she is the one who helped me to fall in love with reading, writing, and being creative, and most likely where I get the majority of my creativity.

"Be the water in the desert that brings the beauty and wonder back to life"

About The Author

Robert Knott was born in Houston, TX. He graduated from Texas State University with a bachelor's of science in psychology. His art and literary work explores the topics of birth, death, pain, loss, creation, nature, and the alchemy of transmutation in relation to love and growth.